The Heavenly Life

JAMES ALLEN

Author of "AS A MAN THINKETH"

Foreword by
Roy Eugene Davis

CSA PRESS
LAKEMONT, GEORGIA 30552

Standard Book Number 0-87707-151-9

Photograph for cover copyright by Icelandic Photo and Press Service. Mats Wibe Lund, Jr., photographer, Reykjavik, Iceland.

Printed in the United States of America
by CSA Printing and Bindery, Inc.

3V
+501
A56
1975

CONTENTS

FOREWORD

"Wisdom is found only by constant practice in pure thinking and well-doing; by harmonizing one's mind and heart to those things which are beautiful, lovable, and true."

James Allen had the rare gift of saying in a few words, what we all know so well in the depths of our own being. There is no need to attempt to add to his message; for it is quite complete and serves well the purpose of bringing us back to the basic essentials. Life need not be complicated. All that is required is for one to quietly contemplate the *natural order of things* until the truth is Self-revealed from within. This is one of the keys to receiving the most benefit from this booklet—to relax the conscious mind and allow understanding and grace to surface.

—Roy Eugene Davis

THE DIVINE CENTER

The secret of life, of abundant life, with its strength, its felicity, and its unbroken peace is to find the Divine Center within oneself, and to live in and from that, instead of in that outer circumference of disturbances—the clamors, cravings, and argumentations which make up the animal and intellectual man. These selfish elements constitute the mere husks of life, and must be thrown away by him who would penetrate to the Central Heart of things—to Life itself.

Not to know that within you which is changeless, and defiant of time and death, is not to know anything, but is to play vainly with unsubstantial reflections in the Mirror of Time. Not to find within you those passionless Principles which are not moved by the strifes and shows and vanities of the world, is to find nothing but illusions which vanish as they are grasped.

He who resolves that he will not rest satisfied with appearances, shadows, illusions shall, by the piercing light of that resolve, disperse every fleet-

ing fantasy, and shall enter into the substance and
reality of life. He shall learn how to live, and he
shall *live*. He shall be the slave of no passion, the
servant of no opinion, the votary of no fond error.
Finding the Divine with his own heart, he will
ceaselessly radiate the Heavenly Life in which he
lives—*which is himself*.

Having betaken himself to the Divine Refuge
within, and remaining there, a man is free from
sin. All his yesterdays are as the tide-washed and
untrodden sands; no sin shall rise up against him
to torment and accuse him and destroy his sacred
peace; the fires of remorse cannot scorch him,
nor can the storms of regret devastate his dwelling-place. His tomorrows are as seeds which
shall germinate, bursting into beauty and potency
of life, and no doubt shall shake his trust, no uncertainty rob him of repose. The *Present* is his,
only in the immortal Present does he live, and it
is as the eternal vault of blue above which looks
down silently and calmly, yet radiant with purity
and light, upon the upturned and tear-stained
faces of the centuries.

Men love their desires, for gratification seems
sweet to them, but its end is pain and vacuity;
they love the argumentations of the intellect, for
egotism seems most desirable to them, but the
fruits thereof are humiliation and sorrow. When
the soul has reached the end of gratification and
reaped the bitter fruits of egotism, it is ready to
receive the Divine Wisdom and to enter into the
Divine Life, Only the crucified can be transfig-
ured; only by the death of self can the Lord of the
heart rise again into the Immortal Life, and stand
radiant upon the Olivet of Wisdom.

Thou hast thy trials? Every outward trial is the replica of an inward imperfection. Thou shalt grow wise by knowing this, and shalt thereby transmute trial into active joy, finding the Kingdom where trial cannot come. When wilt thou learn thy lessons, O child of earth! All thy sorrows cry out against thee; every pain is thy just accuser, and thy griefs are but the shadows of thy unworthy and perishable self. The Kingdom of Heaven is thine; how long wilt thou reject it, preferring the lurid atmosphere of Hell—the hell of thy self-seeking self?

Where self is not there is the Garden of the Heavenly Life, and

"There spring the healing streams
    Quenching all thirst! there bloom the immortal
        flowers
Carpeting all the way with joy! there throng
    Swiftest and sweetest hours!"

The redeemed sons of God, the glorified in body and spirit, are "bought with a price," and that price is the crucifixion of the personality, the death of self; and having put away that within which is the source of all discord, they have found the universal Music, the abiding Joy.

Life is more than motion, it is Music; more than rest, it is Peace; more than work, it is Duty; more than labor, it is Love; more than enjoyment, it is Blessedness; more than acquiring money and position and reputation, it is Knowledge, Purpose, strong and high Resolve.

Let the impure turn to Purity, and they shall be pure; let the weak resort to Strength, and they shall be strong; let the ignorant fly to Knowledge, and they shall be wise. All things are man's, and he chooses that which he will have. Today he chooses in ignorance, tomorrow he shall choose in Wisdom. He shall "work out his own salvation" whether he believe it or not, for he cannot escape himself, nor transfer to another the eternal responsibility of his own soul. By no theological subterfuge shall he trick the Law of his being, which shall shatter all his selfish makeshifts and excuses for right thinking and right doing. Nor shall God do for him that which it is destined his soul shall accomplish for itself. What would you say of a man who, wanting to possess a mansion in which to dwell peacefully, purchased the site and then knelt down and asked God to build the house for him? Would you not say that such a man was foolish? And of another man who, having purchased the land, set the architects and builders and carpenters at work to erect the edifice, would you not say that he was wise? And as it is in the building of a material house, even so it is in the building of a spiritual mansion. Brick by brick, pure thought upon pure thought, good deed upon good deed, must the habitation of a blameless life rise from its sure foundation until at last it stands out in all the majesty of its faultless proportions. Not by caprice, nor gift, nor favor does a man obtain the spiritual realities, but by diligence, watchfulness, energy, and effort.

"Strong is the soul, and wise and beautiful;
The seeds of God-like power are in us still;
Gods are we, bards, saints, heroes, if we will."

The Spiritual Heart of man is the Heart of the universe, and, finding that Heart, man finds the strength to accomplish all things. He finds there also the Wisdom to see things as they are. He finds there the Peace that is divine. At the center of man's being is the Music which orders the stars —the Eternal Harmony. He who would find Blessedness, let him find himself; let him abandon every discordant desire, every inharmonious thought, every unlovely habit and deed, and he will find that Grace and Beauty and Harmony which form the indestructible essence of his own being.

Men fly from creed to creed, and find—unrest; they travel in many lands, and discover—disappointment; they build themselves beautiful mansions, and plant pleasant gardens, and reap—ennui and discomfort. Not until a man falls back upon the Truth within himself does he find rest and satisfaction; not until he builds the inward Mansion of Faultless Conduct does he find the endless and incorruptible Joy, and, having obtained that, he will infuse it into all his outward doings and possessions.

If a man would have peace, let him exercise the spirit of Peace; if he would find love, let him dwell in the spirit of Love; if he would escape suffering, let him cease to inflict it; if he would do noble things for humanity, let him cease to do ignoble things for himself. If he will but quarry the mine of his own soul, he shall find there all the materials for building whatsoever he will, and he shall find there also the central Rock on which to build in safety.

Howsoever a man works to right the world, it will never be righted until he has put himself right. This may be written upon the heart as a mathematical axiom. It is not enough to preach Purity, men must cease from lust; to exhort to love, they must abandon hatred; to extol self-sacrifice, they must yield up self; to adorn with mere words the Perfect Life, they must *be* perfect.

When a man can no longer carry the weight of his many sins, let him fly to the Christ, whose throne is the center of his own heart, and he shall become light-hearted, entering the glad company of the Immortals.

When he can no longer bear the burden of his accumulated learning, let a man leave his books, his science, his philosophy, and come back to himself, and he shall find within, that which he outwardly sought and found not—his own divinity.

He ceases to argue about God who has found God within. Relying upon that calm strength which is not the strength of self, he *lives* God, manifesting in his daily life the Highest Goodness, which is Eternal Life.

THE ETERNAL NOW

Now is the reality in which time is contained. It is more and greater than time; it is an ever-present reality. It knows neither past nor future, and is eternally potent and substantial. Every minute, every day, every year is a dream as soon as it has passed, and exists only as an imperfect and unsubstantial picture in the memory, if it be not entirely obliterated.

Past and future are dreams; *now* is a reality. All things are now; all power, all possibility, all action is now. Not to act and accomplish now is not to act and accomplish at all. To live in thoughts of what you might have done, or in dreams of what you mean to do, this is folly; but to put away regret, to anchor anticipation, and to do and to work *now*, this is wisdom.

Whilst a man is dwelling upon the past or future he is missing the present; he is forgetting to live now. All things are possible now, and *only* now. Without wisdom to guide him, and mistaking the unreal for the real, a man says, "If I had done

so and so last week, last month, or last year, it
would have been better with me today"; or, "I
know what is best to be done, and I will do it tomorrow." The selfish cannot comprehend the
vast importance and value of the present, and
fail to see it as the substantial reality of which
past and future are the empty reflections. It may
truly be said that past and furure do not exist
except as negative shadows, and to live in them—
that is, in the regretful and selfish contemplation
of them—is to miss the reality in life.

"The Present, the Present is all thou hast
    For thy sure possessing;
Like the patriarch's angel, hold it fast,
    Till it gives its blessing.

"All which is real now remaineth,
    And fadeth never:
The hand which upholds it now sustaineth
    The soul forever.

"Then of what is to be, and of what is done,
    Why queriest thou?
The past and the time to be are one,
    And both are NOW!"

Man has all power now; but not knowing this,
he says, "I will be perfect next year, or in so many
years, or in so many lives." The dwellers in the
Kingdom of God, who live only in the now, say,
"I am perfect now," and refraining from all sin
now, and ceaselessly guarding the portals of the
mind, not looking to the past nor to the future,

nor turning to the left or right, they remain eternally holy and blessed. "Now is the accepted time; now is the day of salvation."

Say to yourself, "I will live in my Ideal now; I will manifest my Ideal now; I will be my Ideal now; and all that tempts me away from my Ideal I will not listen to; I will listen only to the voice of my Ideal." Thus resolving, and thus doing, you shall not depart from the Highest, and shall eternally manifest the True.

"Afoot and lighthearted, I take to the open road.
Henceforth I ask not good fortune: I myself am good fortune.
Henceforth I whimper no more, postpone no more, need nothing;
Done with indoor complaints, libraries, querulous criticisms.
Strong and content, I take to the open road."

Cease to tread every byway of dependence, every winding side-way that tempts thy soul into shadow-land of the past and the future, and manifest thy native and divine strength now. Come out into "the open road."

That which you would be, and hope to be, you may be now. Non-accomplishment resides in your perpetual postponement, and, having the power to postpone, you also have the power to accomplish—to perpetually accomplish. Realize this truth, and you shall be today; and every day, the ideal man of whom you dreamed.

Virtue consists in fighting sin day after day, but holiness consists in leaving sin, unnoticed and ignored. to die by the wayside, and this is done, can only be done, in the living now. Say not unto thy soul, "Thou shalt be purer tomorrow"; but rather say, "Thou shalt be pure now." Tomorrow is too late for anything, and he who sees his help and salvation in tomorrow shall continually fail and fall today.

Thou didst fall yesterday? Didst sin grievously? Having realized this, leave it instantly and forever, and watch that thou sinnest not now. The while thou art bewailing the past every gate of thy soul remains unguarded against the entrance of sin now. Thou shalt not rise by grieving over the irremediable past, but by remedying the present.

The foolish man, loving the boggy sidepath of procrastination rather than the firm Highway of Present Effort, says, "I will rise early tomorrow; I will get out of debt tomorrow; I will carry out my intentions tomorrow." But the wise man, realizing the momentous import of the Eternal Now, rises early today; keeps out of debt today; carries out his intentions today; and so never departs from strength and peace and ripe accomplishment.

That which is done now remains; that which is to be done tomorrow does not appear. It is wisdom to leave that which has not arrived, and to attend to that which is; and to attend to it with such a consecration of soul and concentration of effort as shall leave no possible loophole for regret to creep in.

A man's spiritual comprehension being clouded by the illusions of self, he says, "I was born on such a day, so many years ago, and shall die at my allotted time." But he was not born, neither will he die, for how can that which is immortal, which eternally *is,* be subject to birth and death? Let a man throw off his illusions, and then he will see that the birth and death of the *body* are the mere incidents of a journey, and not its beginning and end.

Looking back to happy beginnings, and forward to mournful endings, a man's eyes are blinded, so that he beholds not his own immortality; his ears are closed, so that he hears not the ever-present harmonies of Joy; and his heart is hardened, so that it pulsates not to the rhythmic sounds of Peace.

The universe, with all that it contains, is now. Put out thy hand, O man, and receive the fruits of Wisdom! Cease from thy greedy striving, thy selfish sorrowing, thy foolish regretting, and be content to *live.* Act now, and, lo! all things are done; live now, and, behold! thou art in the midst of Plenty; *be* now, and *know* that thou art perfect.

THE "ORIGINAL SIMPLICITY"

Life is simple. Being is simple. The universe is simple. Complexity arises in ignorance and self-delusion. The "Original Simplicity" of Laotze is a term expressive of the universe at it *is*, and not as it *appears*. Looking through the woven network of his own illusions, man sees interminable complication and unfathomable mystery, and so loses himself in the labyrinths of his own making. Let a man put away egotism, and he will see the universe in all the beauty of its pristine simplicity. Let him annihilate the delusion of the personal "I," and he will destroy all the illusions which spring from that "I." He will thus "re-become a little child," and will "revert to Original Simplicity."

When a man succeeds in entirely forgetting (annihilating) his personal self, he becomes a mirror in which the universal Reality is faultlessly reflected. He is awakened, and henceforward he lives, not in dreams, but realities.

Pythagoras saw the universe in the ten numbers, but even this simplicity may be further reduced, and the universe ultimately be found to be contained in the number ONE, for all the numerals and all their infinite complications are but additions of the *One*.

Let life cease to be lived as a fragmentary thing, and let it be lived as a perfect Whole; the simplicity of the Perfect will then be revealed. How shall the fragment comprehend the Whole? Yet how simple that the Whole should comprehend the fragment. How shall sin perceive Holiness? Yet how plain that Holiness should understand sin. He who would become the Greater let him abandon the lesser. In no form is the circle contained, but in the circle all forms are contained. In no color is the radiant light imprisoned, but in the radiant light all colors are embodied. Let a man destroy all the forms of self, and he shall apprehend the Circle of Perfection; let him submerge in the silent depths of his being, the varying colors of his thoughts and desires, and he shall be illuminated with the White Light of Divine Knowledge. In the perfect chord of music the single note, though forgotten, is indispensably contained, and the drop of water becomes of supreme usefulness by losing itself in the ocean. Sink thyself compassionately in the heart of humanity, and thou shalt reproduce the harmonies of Heaven; lose thyself in unlimited love toward all, and thou shalt work enduring works and shalt become one with the eternal Ocean of Bliss.

Man evolves outward to the periphery of complexity, and then involves backward to the Central Simplicity. When a man discovers that it is mathematically impossible for him to know the universe before knowing himself, he then starts upon the Way which leads to the Original Simplicity. He begins to unfold from within, and as he unfolds himself, he enfolds the universe.

Cease to speculate about God, and find the all-embracing Good within thee, then shalt thou see the emptiness and vanity of speculation knowing thyself one with God.

He who will not give up his secret lust, his covetousness, his anger, his opinion about this or that, can see nor know nothing; he will remain a dullard in the school of Wisdom, though he be accounted learned in the colleges.

If a man would find the Key of Knowledge, let him find himself. Thy sins are not thyself; they are not any part of thyself; they are diseases which thou hast come to love. Cease to cling to them, and they will no longer cling to thee. Let them fall away, and thy self shall stand revealed. Thou shalt then know thyself as Comprehensive Vision, Invincible Principle, Immortal Life, and Eternal Good.

The impure man believes impurity to be his rightful condition, but the pure man knows himself as pure being; he also, penetrating the Veils, sees all others as pure being. Purity is extremely simple, and needs no argument to support it; impurity is interminably complex, and is ever involved in defensive argument. Truth *lives* itself. A blameless life is the only witness of Truth. Men cannot see, and will not accept the witness until they find it within themselves; and having found it, a man becomes silent before his fellows. Truth is so simple that it cannot be found in the region of argument and advertisement, and so silent that it is only manifested in actions.

So extremely simple is Original Simplicity, that a man must let go his hold of everything before he can perceive it. The great arch is strong by virtue of the hollowness underneath, and a wise man becomes strong and invincible by emptying himself.

Meekness, Patience, Love, Compassion, and Wisdom—these are the dominant qualities of Original Simplicity; therefore the imperfect cannot understand it. Wisdom only can apprehend Wisdom, therefore the fool says, "No man is wise." The imperfect man says, "No man can be perfect," and he therefore remains where he is. Though he live with a perfect man all his life, he shall not behold his perfection. Meekness he will call cowardice; Patience, Love, and Compassion he will see as weakness; and Wisdom will appear to him as folly. Faultless discrimination belongs to the Perfect Whole, and resides not in any part, therefore men are exhorted to refrain from judgment until they have themselves manifested the Perfect Life.

Arriving at Original Simplicity, opacity disappears, and the universal transparency becomes apparent. He who has found the indwelling Reality of his own being has found the original and universal Reality. Knowing the Divine Heart within, all hearts are known, and the thoughts of

all men become his who has become the master of
his own thoughts; therefore the good man does
not defend himself, but moulds the minds of
others to his own likeness.

As the problematical transcends crudity, so
Pure Goodness transcends the problematical. All
problems vanish when Pure Goodness is reached;
therefore the good man is called "The slayer of
illusions." What problem can vex where sin is
not? O thou who strivest loudly and retest not!
retire into the holy silence of thine own being, and
live therefrom. So shalt thou, finding Pure Goodness, rend in twain the Veil of the Temple of Illusion, and shalt enter into the Patience, Peace,
and transcendent Glory of the Perfect, for Pure
Goodness and Original Simplicity are one.

THE UNFAILING WISDOM

A man should be superior to his possessions, his body, his circumstances and surroundings, and the opinions of others and their attitude towards him. Until he is this, he is not strong and steadfast. He should also rise superior to his own desires and opinions; and until he is this, he is not wise.

The man who identifies himself with his possessions will feel that all is lost when they are lost; he who regards himself as the outcome and the tool of circumstances will weakly fluctuate with every change in his outward condition; and great will be his unrest and pain who seeks to stand upon the approbation of others.

To detach oneself from every outward thing and to rest securely upon the inward Virtue, this is the Unfailing Wisdom. Having this Wisdom, a man will be the same whether in riches or poverty. The one cannot add to his strength, nor the other rob him of his serenity. Neither can riches defile him who has washed away all the inward defilement, nor the lack of them degrade him who has ceased to degrade the temple of his soul.

To refuse to be enslaved by any outward thing or happening, regarding all such things and happenings as for your use, for your education, this is Wisdom. To the wise all occurrences are *good,* and, having no eye for evil, they grow wiser every day. They utilize all things, and thus put all things under their feet. They see all their mistakes as soon as made, and accept them as lessons of intrinsic value, knowing that there are no mistakes in the Divine Order. They thus rapidly approach the Divine Perfection. They are moved by none, yet learn from all. They crave love from none, yet give love to all. To learn, and not to be shaken; to love where one is not loved; herein lies the strength which shall never fail a man. The man who says in his heart, "I will teach all men, and learn from none," will neither teach nor learn whilst he is in that frame of mind, but will remain in his folly.

All strength and wisdom and power and knowledge a man will find within himself, but he will not find it in egotism; he will only find it in obedience, submission, and willingness to learn. He must obey the Higher, and not glorify himself in the lower. He who stands upon egotism, rejecting reproof, instruction, and the lessons of experience, will surely fall; yea, he is already fallen. Said a great Teacher to his disciples, "Those who shall be a lamp unto themselves, relying upon themselves only, and not relying upon any external help, but holding fast to the Truth as their lamp, and, seeking their salvation in the Truth alone, shall not look for assistance to any besides themselves, it is they among my disciples who shall reach the very topmost height! *But they must be willing to learn.''* The wise man is always anxious to learn, but never anxious to teach, for he knows that the true Teacher is in the heart of every man, and must ultimately be found there by all. The foolish man, being governed largely by vanity, is very anxious to teach, but unwilling to learn, not having found the Holy Teacher within who speaks wisdom to the humbly listening soul. Be self-reliant, but let thy self-reliance be saintly and not selfish.

Folly and wisdom, weakness and strength are within a man, and not in any external thing, neither do they spring from any external cause. A man cannot be strong for another, he can only be strong for himself; he cannot overcome for another, he can only overcome of himself. You may learn of another, but you must accomplish for yourself. Put away all external props, and rely upon the Truth within you. A creed will not bear a man up in the hour of temptation; he must possess the inward Knowledge which slays temptation. A speculative philosophy will prove a shadowy thing in the time of calamity; a man must have the inward Wisdom which puts an end to grief.

Goodness, which is the aim of all religions, is distinct from religions themselves. Wisdom, which is the aim of every philosophy, is distinct from all philosophies. The Unfailing Wisdom is found only by constant practice in pure thinking and well-doing; by harmonizing one's mind and heart to those things which are beautiful, lovable, and true.

In whatever condition a man finds himself, he can always find the True; and he can find it only by so utilizing his present condition as to become strong and wise. The effeminate hankering after rewards, and the craven fear of punishment, let them be put away forever, and let a man joyfully bend himself to the faithful performance of all his duties, forgetting himself and his worthless pleasures, and living strong and pure and self-contained; so shall he surely find the Unfailing Wisdom, the God-like Patience and strength. "The situation that has not its Duty, its Ideal, was never yet occupied by man . . . . Here or nowhere is thy Ideal. Work it out therefrom, and, working, believe, live, be free. The Ideal is in thyself, the impediment, too, is in thyself; thy condition is but the stuff thou art to shape that same Ideal out of. What matter whether such stuff be of this sort or that, so the form thou give it be heroic, be poetic? Oh, thou that pinest in the imprisonment of the Actual, and criest bitterly to the gods for a kingdom wherein to rule and create, know this of a truth: the thing thou seekest is already within thee, here and now, couldst thou only see!"

All that is beautiful and blessed is in thyself, not in thy neighbor's wealth. Thou art poor? Thou art poor indeed if thou are not stronger than thy poverty! Thou hast suffered calamities? Well, wilt thou cure calamity by adding anxiety to it? Canst thou mend a broken vase by weeping over it, or restore a lost delight by thy lamentations? There is no evil but will vanish if thou wilt wisely meet it. The God-like soul does not grieve over that which has been, is, or will be, but perpetually finds the Divine Good, and gains wisdom by every occurrence.

Fear is the shadow of selfishness, and cannot live where loving Wisdom is. Doubt, anxiety, and worry are unsubstantial shades in the underworld of self, and shall no more trouble him who will climb the serene altitudes of his soul. Grief, also, will be forever dispelled by him who will comprehend the Law of his being. He who so comprehends shall find the Supreme Law of Life, and he shall find that it is Love, that it is imperishable Love. He shall become one with that Love, and loving all, with mind freed from all hatred and folly, he shall receive the invincible protection which Love affords. Claiming nothing, he shall suffer no loss; seeking no pleasure, he shall find no grief; and employing all his powers as instruments of service, he shall evermore live in the highest state of blessedness and bliss.

Know this:—thou makest and unmakest thyself; thou standest and fallest by what thou art. Thou art a slave if thou preferrest to be; thou art a master if thou wilt make thyself one. Build upon thy animal desires and intellectual opinions, and thou buildest upon the sand; build upon Virtue and Holiness, and no wind nor tide shall shake thy strong abode. So shall the Unfailing Wisdom uphold thee in every emergency, and the Everlasting Arms gather thee to thy peace.

> "Lay up each year
> Thy harvest of well-doing, wealth that kings
> Nor thieves can take away. When all the things
> Thou callest thine, goods, pleasures, honors fall,
> Thou in thy virtue shalt survive them all."

THE MIGHT OF MEEKNESS

The mountain bends not to the fiercest storm, but it shields the fledgling and the lamb; and though all men tread upon it, yet it protects them, and bears them up upon its deathless bosom. Even so is it with the meek man who, though shaken and disturbed by none, yet compassionately bends to shield the lowliest creature, and, though he may be despised, lifts all men up, and lovingly protects them.

As glorious as the mountain in its silent might is the divine man in his silent Meekness; like its form, his loving comparison is expansive and sublime. Truly his body, like the mountain's base, is fixed in the valleys and the mists; but the summit of his being is eternally bathed in cloudless glory, and lives with the Silences.

He who has found Meekness has found divinity; he has realized the divine consciousness, and knows himself as divine. He also knows all others as divine, though they know it not themselves, being asleep and dreaming. Meekness is a divine quality, and as such is all-powerful. The meek man overcomes by not resisting, and by allowing himself to be defeated he attains to the Supreme Conquest.

The man who conquers another by force is strong; the man who conquers himself by Meekness is mighty. He who conquers another by force will himself likewise by conquered; he who conquers himself by Meekness will never be overthrown, for the human cannot overcome the divine. The meek man is triumphant in defeat. Socrates lives the more by being put to death; in the crucified Jesus the risen Christ is revealed, and Stephen in receiving his stoning defies the hurting power of stones. That which is real cannot be destroyed, but only that which is unreal. When a man finds that within him which is real, which is constant, abiding, changeless, and eternal, he enters into that Reality, and becomes meek. All the powers of darkness will come against him, but they will do him no hurt, and will at last depart from him.

The meek man is found in the time of trial; when other men fall he stands. His patience is not destroyed by the foolish passions of others, and when they come against him he does not "strive nor cry." He knows the utter powerlessness of all evil, having overcome it in himself, and lives in the changeless strength and power of divine Good.

Meekness is one aspect of the operation of that changeless Love which is at the Heart of all things, and is therefore an imperishable quality. He who lives in it is without fear, knowing the Highest, and having the lowest under his feet.

The meek man shines in darkness, and flourishes in obscurity. Meekness cannot boast, nor advertise itself, nor thrive on popularity. It is *practiced,* and is seen or not seen; being a spiritual quality it is perceived only by the eye of the spirit. Those who are not spiritually awakened see it not, nor do they love it, being enamored of, and blinded by, worldly shows and appearances. Nor does history take note of the meek man. Its glory is that of strife and self-aggrandizement; his is the glory of peace and gentleness. History chronicles the earthly, not the heavenly acts. Yet though he lives in obscurity he cannot be hidden (how can light be hid?); he continues to shine after he has withdrawn himself from the world, and is worshipped by the world which knew him not.

That the meek man should be neglected, abused, or misunderstood is reckoned by him as of no account, and therefore not to be considered, much less resisted. He knows that all such weapons are the flimsiest and most ineffectual of shadows. To them, therefore, who give him evil he gives good. He resists none, and thereby conquers all.

He who imagines he can be injured by others, and who seeks to justify and defend himself against them, does not understand Meekness, does not comprehend the essence and meaning of life. "He abused me, he beat me, he defeated me, he robbed me." In those who harbor such thoughts hatred will never cease . . . for hatred ceases not by hatred at any time; hatred ceases by love. What sayest thou, thy neighbor has spoken thee falsely? Well, what of that? Can a falsity hurt thee? That which is false is false, and there is an end of it. It is without life, and without power to hurt any but him who seeks to be hurt by it. It is nothing to thee that thy neighbor should speak falsely of thee, but it is much to thee that thou shouldst resist him, and seek to justify thyself, for, by so doing, thou givest life and vitality to thy neighbor's falseness, so that thou are injured and distressed. Take all evil out of thine own heart, then shalt thou see the folly of resisting it in another. Thou wilt be trodden on? Thou are trodden on already if thou thinkest thus. The injury that thou seest as coming from another comes only from thyself. The wrong thought, or word, or act of another has no power to hurt thee unless thou galvanize it into life by the passionate resistance, and so receivest it into thyself. If any man slander me, that is his concern, not mine. I have to do with my own soul, not with my neighbor's. Though all the world misjudge me, it is no business of mine; but that I should possess my soul in Purity and Love, that is all my business. There shall be no end to strife until men cease to justify themselves. He who would have wars cease let him cease to defend any party— let him cease to defend himself. Not by strife can peace come, but by ceasing from strife. The glory of Caesar resides in the resistance of his enemies. They resist and fall. Give to Caesar that which Caesar demands, and Caesar's glory and power are gone. Thus, by submission does the meek man conquer the strong man; but it is not that outward show of submission which is slavery, it is that inward and spiritual submission which is *freedom.*

Claiming no *rights,* the meek man is not troubled with self-defense and self-justification; he lives in love, and therefore comes under the immediate and vital protection of the Great Love which is the Eternal Law of the universe. He neither claims nor seeks his own; thus do all things come to him, and all the universe shields and protects him.

He who says, "I have tried Meekness, and it has failed," has not tried Meekness. It cannot be tried as an experiment. It is only arrived at by unreserved self-sacrifice. Meekness does not consist merely in non-resistance in *thought,* in ceasing to hold or to have any selfish, condemnatory, or retaliatory thoughts. The meek man, therefore, cannot "Take offense" or have his "feelings hurt," living above hatred, folly, and vanity. Meekness can never fail.

O thou who searchest for the Heavenly Life! strive after Meekness; increase thy patience and forbearance day by day; bid thy tongue cease from all harsh words, withdraw thy mind from selfish arguments, and refuse to brood upon thy wrongs: so living, thou shalt carefully tend and cultivate the pure and delicate flower of Meekness in thy heart, until at last, its divine sweetness and purity and beauteous perfection shall be revealed to thee, and thou shalt become gentle, joyful, and strong. Repine not that thou art surrounded by irritable and selfish people; but rather rejoice that thou are so favored as to have thine own imperfections revealed to thee, and that thou art so placed as to necessitate within thee a constant struggle for self-mastery and the attainment of perfection. The more there is of harshness and selfishness around thee the greater is the need of thy Meekness and love. If others seek to wrong thee, all the more is it needful that thou shouldst cease from all wrong, and live in love; if others preach Meekness, humility, and love, and do not practice these, trouble not, nor be annoyed; but do thou, in the silence of thy heart, and in thy contact with others, *practice* these things, and they shall preach themselves. And though thou utter no declamatory word, and stand before no gathered audience, thou shalt teach the whole world. As thou becomest meek, thou shalt learn the deepest secrets of the universe. Nothing is hidden from him who overcomes himself. Into the cause of causes shalt thou penetrate, and lifting, one after another, every veil of illusion, shalt reach at last the inmost Heart of Being. Thus becoming one with Life, thou shalt know all life, and, seeing into causes, and knowing realities, thou shalt be no more anxious about thyself, and others, and the world, but shalt see that all things that are are engines of the Great Law. Canopied with gentleness, thou shalt bless where others curse; love where others hate; forgive where others condemn; yield where others strive; give up where others grasp; lose where others gain. And in their strength they shall be weak; and in thy weakness thou shalt be strong; yea, thou shalt mightily prevail. He that hath not unbroken gentleness hath not Truth:

"Therefore when Heaven would save a man, it enfolds him with gentlensss."

THE RIGHTEOUS MAN

The righteous man is invincible. No enemy can possibly overcome or confound him; and he needs no other protection than that of his own integrity and holiness.

As it is impossible for evil to overcome Good, so the righteous man can never be brought low by the unrighteous. Slander, envy, hatred, malice can never reach him, nor cause him any suffering, and those who try to injure him only succeed ultimately in bringing ignominy upon themselves.

The righteous man, having nothing to hide, committing no acts which require stealth, and harboring no thoughts and desires which he would not like others to know, is fearless and unashamed. His step is firm, his body upright, and his speech direct and without ambiguity. He looks everybody in the face. How can he fear any who wrongs none? How can he be ashamed before any who deceives none? And ceasing from all wrong he can never be deceived.

The righteous man, performing all his duties with scrupulous diligence, and living above sin, is invulnerable at every point. He who has slain the inward enemies of virtue can never be brought low by any outward enemy; neither does he need to seek any protection against them, righteousness being an all-sufficient protection.

The unrighteous man is vulnerable at almost every point; living in his passions, the slave of prejudices, impulses, and ill-formed opinions, he is continually suffering (as he imagines) at the hands of others. The slanders, attacks, and accusations of others cause him great suffering because they have a basis of truth in himself; and not having the protection of righteousness, he endeavors to justify and protect himself by resorting to retaliation and specious argument, and even to subterfuge and deceit.

The partially righteous man is vulnerable at all those points where he falls short of righteousness, and should the righteous man fall from his righteousness, and give way to *one* sin, his invincibility is gone, for he has thereby placed himself where attack and accusation can justly reach and injure him, because he has first injured himself.

If a man suffers or is injured through the instrumentality of others, let him look to himself, and, putting aside self-pity and self-defense, he will find in his own heart the source of all his woe.

No evil can happen to the righteous man who has cut off the source of evil in himself; living in the All-Good, and abstaining from sin in thought, word, and deed, whatever happens to him is good; neither can any person, event, or circumstance cause him suffering, for the tyranny of circumstance is utterly destroyed for him who has broken the bonds of sin.

The suffering, the sorrowing, the weary, and broken-hearted ever seek a sorrowless refuge, a haven of perpetual peace. Let such fly to the refuge of the righteous life; let them come now and enter the haven of the sinless state, for sorrow cannot overtake the righteous; suffering cannot reach him who does not waste in self-seeking his spiritual substance; and he cannot be afflicted by weariness and unrest whose heart is at peace with all.

PERFECT LOVE

The Children of Light, who abide in the Kingdom of Heaven, see the universe, and all that it contains, as the manifestation of one Law— the Law of Love. They see Love as the moulding, sustaining, protecting, and perfecting Power immanent in all things animate and inanimate. To them Love is not merely and only a rule of life, it is the Law of Life, it is Life itself. Knowing this, they order their whole life in accordance with Love, not regarding their own personality. By thus practicing obedience to the Highest, to divine Love, they become conscious partakers of the power of Love, and so arrive at perfect Freedom as Masters of Destiny.

The universe is preserved because Love is at the Heart of it. Love is the only preservative power. Whilst there is hatred in the heart of man, he imagines the Law to be cruel, but when his heart is mellowed by Compassion and Love, he perceives that the Law is Infinite Kindness. So kind is the Law that it protects man against his own ignorance. Man, in his puny efforts to subvert the Law by attaching undue importance to his own little personality, brings upon himself such trains of suffering that he is at last compelled, in the depth of his afflictions, to seek for Wisdom; and finding Wisdom, he finds Love, and knows it as the Law of his being, the Law of the universe. Love does not punish; man punishes himself by his own hatred; by striving to preserve evil which has no life by which to preserve itself, and by trying to subvert Love, which can neither be overcome nor destroyed, being of the substance of Life. When a man burns himself, does he accuse the fire? Therefore, when a man suffers, let him look for some ignorance or disobedience within himself.

Love is Perfect Harmony, pure Bliss, and contains, therefore, no element of suffering. Let a man think no thought and do no act which is not in accordance with pure Love, and suffering shall no more trouble him. If a man would know Love, and partake of its undying bliss, he must practice it in his heart; he must become Love.

He who always acts from the spirit of Love is never deserted, is never left in a dilemma or difficulty, for Love (impersonal Love) is both Knowledge and Power. He who has learned how to Love has learned how to master every difficulty, how to transmute every failure into success, how to clothe every event and condition in garments of blessedness and beauty.

The way to Love is by self-mastery, and, traveling that way, a man builds himself up in Knowledge as he proceeds. Arriving at Love, he enters into full possession of body and mind, by right of the divine Power which he has earned.

"Perfect Love casteth out fear." To know Love is to know that there is no harmful power in the whole universe. Even sin itself, which the worldly and unbelieving imagine is so unconquerable, is known as a very weak and perishable thing, that shrinks away and disappears before the compelling power of Good. Perfect Love is perfect Harmlessness. And he who has destroyed, in himself, all thoughts of harm, and all desire to harm, receives the universal protection, and knows himself to be invincible.

Perfect Love is perfect Patience. Anger and irritability cannot dwell with it nor come near it. It sweetens every bitter occasion with the perfume of holiness, and transmutes trial into divine strength. Complaint is foreign to it. He who loves bewails nothing, but accepts all things and conditions as heavenly guests; he is therefore constantly blessed, and sorrow does not overtake him.

Perfect Love is perfect Trust. He who has destroyed the desire to grasp can never be troubled with the fear of loss. Loss and gain are alike foreign to him. Steadfastly maintaining a loving attitude of mind toward all, and pursuing, in the performance of his duties, a constant and loving activity, Love protects him and evermore supplies him in fullest measure with all that he needs.

Perfect Love is perfect Power. The wisely loving heart commands without exercising any authority. All things and all men obey him who obeys the Highest. He thinks, and lo! he has already accomplished! He speaks, and behold! a world hangs upon his simple utterances! He has harmonized his thoughts with the Imperishable

and Unconquerable Forces, and for him weakness
and uncertainty are no more. His every thought
is a purpose; his every act an accomplishment;
he moves with the Great Law, not setting his puny
personal will against it, and he thus becomes a
channel through which the divine Power can flow
in unimpeded and beneficent expression. He has
thus become Power itself.

Perfect Love is perfect Wisdom. The man who
loves all is the man who knows all. Having thor-
oughly learned the lessons of his own heart, he
knows the tasks and trials of other hearts, and
adapts himself to them gently and without osten-
tation. Love illuminates the intellect; without it
the intellect is blind and cold and lifeless. Love
succeeds where the intellect fails; sees where the
intellect is blind; knows where the intellect is
ignorant. Reason is only completed in Love, and is
ultimately absorbed in it. Love is the Supreme
Reality in the universe. and as such it contains
all Truth. Infinite Tenderness enfolds and cherish-
es the universe; therefore is the wise man gentle
and childlike and tender-hearted. He sees that the
one thing which all creatures need is Love, and he
gives unstintingly. He knows that all occasions
require the adjusting power of Love, and he ceases
from harshness.

To the eye of Love all things are revealed, not
as an infinity of complex effects, but in the light
of Eternal Principles, out of which spring all
causes and effects, and back into which they return. "God is Love"; therefore than Love there is
nothing more perfect. He who would find pure
Knowledge let him find pure Love.

Perfect Love is perfect Peace. He who dwells with it has completed his pilgrimage in the underworld of sorrow. With mind calm and heart at rest, he has banished the shadows of grief, and knows the deathless Life.

If thou wouldst perfect thyself in Knowledge, perfect thyself in Love. If thou wouldst reach the Highest, ceaselessly cultivate a loving and compassionate heart.

PERFECT FREEDOM

There is no bondage in the Heavenly Life. There is Perfect Freedom. This is its great glory. This Supreme Freedom is gained only by obedience. He who obeys the Highest cooperates with the Highest, and so masters every force within himself and every condition without. A man may choose the lower and neglect the Higher, but the Higher is never overcome by the lower; herein lies the revelation of Freedom. Let a man choose the Higher and abandon the lower; he shall then establish himself as an Overcomer, and shall realize Perfect Freedom.

To give the reins to inclination is the only slavery; to conquer oneself is the only freedom. The slave to self loves his chains, and will not have one of them broken for fear he would be depriving himself of some cherished delight. He clings to his gratifications and vanities, regarding freedom from them as an empty and undesirable condition. He thus defeats and enslaves himself.

By self-enlightenment is Perfect Freedom found. Whilst a man remains ignorant of himself, of his desires, of his emotions and thoughts, and of the inward causes which mould his life and destiny, having neither control nor understanding of himself, he will remain in bondage to passion, sorrow, suffering, and fluctuating fortune. The Land of Perfect Freedom lies through the Gate of Knowledge.

All outward oppression is but the shadow and effect of the real oppression within. For ages the oppressed have cried for liberty, and a thousand man-made statutes have failed to give it to them. They can give it only to themselves; they shall find it only in obedience to the Divine Statutes which are inscribed upon their hearts. Let them resort to the inward Freedom, and the shadow of oppression shall no more darken the earth. Let men cease to oppress themselves, and no man shall oppress his brother.

Men legislate for an *outward* freedom, yet continue to render such freedom impossible of achievement by fostering an inward condition of enslavement. They thus pursue a shadow without, and ignore the substance within. Man will be free when he is freed from self. All outward forms of bondage and oppression will cease to be when man ceases to be the willing bond-slave of passion, error, and ignorance. Freedom is to the free.

Whilst men cling to weakness they cannot have strength; whilst they love darkness they can receive no light; and so long as they prefer bondage they can enjoy no liberty. Strength, light, and freedom are ready now, and can be had by all who love them, who aspire to them. Freedom does not reside in cooperative aggression, for this will always produce, reactively, cooperative defense—warfare, hatred, party strife, and the destruction of liberty. Freedom resides in individual self-conquest. The emancipation of Humanity is frustrated and withheld by the self-enslavement of the unit. Thou who criest to man and God for liberty, liberate thyself!

The Heavenly Freedom is freedom from passion, from cravings, from opinions, from the tyranny of the flesh, and the tyranny of the intellect—this first, and then all outward freedom, as effect to cause. The Freedom that begins within, and extends outwardly until it embraces the whole man, is an emancipation so complete, all-embracing, and perfect as to leave no galling fetter unbroken. Free thy soul from all sin, and thou shalt walk a freed and fearless man in the midst of a world of fearful slaves; and, seeing thee, many slaves shall take heart and shall join thee in thy glorious freedom.

He who says, "My worldly duties are irksome to me; I will leave them and go into solitude, where I shall be as free as the air," and thinks to gain freedom thus, will find only a harder slavery. The tree of Freedom is rooted in Duty, and he who would pluck its sweet fruits must discover joy in Duty.

Glad-hearted, calm, and ready for all tasks is he who is freed from self. Irksomeness and weariness cannot enter his heart, and his divine strength lightens every burden so that its weight is not felt. He does not run away from Duty with his chains about him, but breaks them and stands free.

Make thyself pure; make thyself proof against weakness, temptation, and sin; for only in thine own heart and mind shalt thou find that Perfect Freedom for which the whole world sighs and seeks in vain.

GREATNESS AND GOODNESS

Goodness, simplicity, greatness—these three are one, and this trinity of perfection cannot be separated. All greatness springs from goodness, and all goodness is profoundly simple. Without goodness there is no greatness. Some men pass through the world as destructive forces, like the tornado or the avalanche, but they are not great; they are to greatness as the avalanche is to the mountain. The work of greatness is enduring and preservative, and not violent and destructive. The greatest souls are the most gentle.

Greatness is never obtrusive. It works in silence, seeking no recognition. This is why it is not easily perceived and recognized. Like the mountain, it towers up in its vastness, so that those in its immediate vicinity, who receive its shelter and shade, do not see it. Its sublime grandeur is only beheld as they recede from it. The great man is not seen by his contemporaries; the majesty of his form is only outlined by its recession in time. This is the awe and enchant-

ment of distance. Men occupy themselves with the
small things; their houses, trees, lands. Few contemplate the mountain at whose base they live,
and fewer still essay to explore it. But in the distance these small things disappear, and then the
solitary beauty of the mountain is perceived. Popularity, noisy obtrusiveness, and shallow show,
these superficialities rapidly disappear, and leave
behind no enduring mark; whereas greatness
slowly emerges from obscurity, and endures forever.

Jewish Rabbi and rabble alike saw not the
divine beauty of Jesus; they saw only an un-
lettered carpenter. To his acquaintances, Homer
was only a blind beggar, but the centuries reveal
him as Homer the immortal poet. Two hundred
years after the farmer of Stratford (and all that
is known of him) has disappeared the *real*
Shakespeare is discerned. All true genius is impersonal. It belongs not to the man through whom
it is manifested; it belongs to all. It is a diffusion
of pure Truth; the Light of Heaven descending
on all mankind.

Every work of genius, in whatsoever depart-
ment of art, is a symbolic manifestation of impersonal Truth. It is universal, and finds a re-
sponse in every heart in every age and race. Anything short of this is not genius, is not greatness.
That work which defends a religion perishes;
it is *religion* that lives. Theories about immortality fade away, immortal man endures; com-
mentaries upon Truth come to the dust; Truth
alone remains. That only is true in art which rep-
resents the True; that only is great in life which

is universally and eternally true. And the True is the Good; the Good is the True.

Every immortal work springs from the Eternal Goodness in the human heart, and it is clothed with the sweet and unaffected simplicity of goodness. The greatest art is, like nature, *artless*. It knows no trick, no pose, no studied effort. There are no stage-tricks in Shakespeare; and he is the greatest of dramatists because he is the *simplest*. The critics, not understanding the wise simplicity of greatness, always condemn the loftiest work. They cannot discriminate between the *childish* and the *childlike*. The True, the Beautiful, the Great, is always childlike, and is perennially fresh and young.

The great man is always the good man; he is always simple. He draws from, nay, lives in, the inexhaustible fountain of divine Goodness within; he inhabits the Heavenly Places; communes with the vanished great ones; lives with the Invisible. He is inspired, and breathes the airs of Heaven.

He who would be great let him learn to be good. He will therefore become great by not seeking greatness. Aiming at greatness a man arrives at nothingness; aiming at nothingness he arrives at greatness. The desire to be great is an indication of littleness, of personal vanity and obtrusiveness. The willingness to disappear from gaze, the utter absence of self-aggrandizement is the witness of greatness.

Littleness seeks and loves authority. Greatness is never authoritative, and it thereby becomes the authority to which the after ages appeal. He who seeks, loses; he who is willing to lose, wins all men. Be thy simple self, thy better self, thy impersonal self, and lo! thou are great! He who selfishly seeks authority shall succeed only in becoming a trembling apologist courting protection behind the back of acknowledged greatness. He who will become the servant of all men, desiring no personal authority, shall live as a man, and shall be called *great*. ''Abide in the simple and noble regions of thy life, obey thy heart, and thou shalt reproduce the foreworld again.'' Forget thine own little self, and fall back upon the Universal self, and thou shalt reproduce, in living and enduring forms, a thousand beautiful experiences; thou shalt find within thyself that simple goodness which is greatness.''

''It is as easy to be great as to be small,'' says Emerson; and he utters a profound truth. Forgetfulness of self is the whole of greatness, as it is the whole of goodness and happiness. In a fleeting moment of self-forgetfulness the smallest soul becomes great; extend that moment indefintely, and there is a great soul, a great life. Cast away thy personality (thy petty cravings, vanities, and ambitions) as a worthless garment, and dwell in the loving, compassionate, selfless regions of thy soul, and thou are no longer small— thou art great.

Claiming personal authority, a man descends into littleness. practicing goodness, a man ascends into greatness. The presumptuousness of the small may, for a time, obscure the humility of the great, but it is at last swallowed up by it, as the noisy river is lost in the calm ocean.

The vulgarity of ignorance and the pride of

learning must disappear. Their worthlessness is equal. They have no part in the Soul of Goodness. If thou wouldst do, thou must *be*. Thou shalt not mistake information for Knowledge; thou must know thy self as pure Knowledge. Thou shalt not confuse learning with Wisdom; thou must apprehend thyself as undefiled Wisdom.

Wouldst thou write a living book? Thou must first *live;* thou shalt draw around thee the mystic garment of a manifold experience, and shalt learn, in enjoyment and suffering, gladness and sorrow, conquest and defeat, that which no book and no teacher can teach thee. Thou shalt learn of life, of thy soul; thou shalt tread the Lonely Road, and shalt *become;* thou shalt *be*. Thou shalt then write thy book, and it shall live; it shall be more than a book. Let thy book first live in thee, then shalt thou live in thy book.

Wouldst thou carve a statue that shall captivate the ages, or paint a picture that shall endure? Thou shalt acquaint thyself with the divine Beauty within thee. Thou shalt comprehend and adore the Invisible Beauty; thou shalt know the Principles which are the soul of form; thou shalt perceive the matchless symmetry and faultless proportions of Life, of Being, of the Universe; thus knowing the eternally True thou shalt carve or paint the indescribably Beautiful.

Wouldst thou produce an imperishable poem? Thou shalt first live thy poem; thou shalt think and act rhythmically; thou shalt find the never-failing source of inspiration in the loving places of thy heart. Then shall immortal lines flow from thee without effort, and, as the flowers of wood and field spontaneously spring, so shall beautiful thoughts grow up in thine heart and, enshrined in words as moulds to their beauty, shall subdue the hearts of men.

Wouldst thou compose such music as shall gladden and uplift the world? Thou shalt adjust thy soul to the Heavenly Harmonies. Thou shalt know that thyself, that life and the universe is Music. Thou shalt touch the chords of Life. Thou shalt know that Music is everywhere; that it is the Heart of Being; then shalt thou hear with thy spiritual ear the Deathless Symphonies.

Wouldst thou preach the living word? Thou shalt forego thyself, and become that Word. Thou shalt know one thing—*that the human heart is good, is divine;* thou shalt live one thing—*Love.* Thou shalt love all, seeing no evil, thinking no evil, believing no evil; then, though thou speak but little, thy every act shall be a power, thy every word a precept. By thy pure thought, thy selfless deed, though it appear hidden, thou shalt preach, down the ages, to untold multitudes of aspiring souls.

To him who chooses Goodness, sacrificing all, is given that which is more than and includes all. He becomes the possessor of the Best, communes with the Highest, and enters the company of the Great.

The greatness that is flawless, rounded, and complete is above and beyond all art. It is Perfect Goodness in manifestation; therefore thy greatest souls are always Teachers.

HEAVEN IN THE HEART

The toil of life ceases when the heart is pure. When the mind is harmonized with the divine Law the wheel of drudgery ceases to turn, and all work is transmuted into joyful activity. The pure-hearted are as the lilies of the field, which toil not, yet are fed and clothed from the abundant storehouse of the All-Good. But the lily is not lethargic; it is ceaselessly active, drawing nourishment from earth and air and sun. By the Divine Power immanent within it, it builds itself up, cell by cell, opening itself to the light, growing and expanding towards the perfect flower. So is it with those who, having yielded up self-will, have learned to cooperate with the Divine Will. They grow in grace, goodness, and beauty, freed from anxiety, and without friction and toil. And they never work in vain; there is no waste action. Every thought, act, and thing done subserves the Divine Purpose, and adds to the sum-total of the world's happiness.

Heaven is in the heart. They will look for it in vain who look elsewhere. In no outward place will the soul find Heaven until it finds it within itself; for, wherever the soul goes, its thoughts and desires will go with it; and, howsoever beautiful may be its outward dwelling-place, if there is sin within, there will be darkness and gloom without, for sin always casts a dark shadow over the pathway of the soul—the shadow of sorrow.

This world is beautiful, transcendently and wonderfully beautiful. Its beauties and inspiring wonders cannot be numbered; yet, to the sin-sodden mind, it appears as a dark and joyless place. Where passion and self are, there is hell, and there are all the pains of hell; where Holiness and Love are, there is Heaven, and there are all the joys of Heaven.

Heaven is here. It is also everywhere. It is wherever there is a pure heart. The whole universe is abounding with joy, but the sin-bound heart can neither see, hear, nor partake of it. No one is, or can be, arbitrarily shut out from Heaven; each shuts himself out. Its Golden Gates are eternally ajar, but the selfish cannot find them; they mourn, yet see not; they cry, but hear not. Only to those who turn their eyes to heavenly things, their ears to heavenly sounds, are the happy Portals of the Kingdom revealed, and they enter and are glad.

All life is gladness when the heart is right, when it is attuned to the sweet chords of holy Love. Life is Religion, Religion is life, and all is Joy and Gladness. The jarring notes of creeds and parties, the black shadows of sin, let them pass away forever; they cannot enter the Door of Life; they form no part of Religion. Joy, Music, Beauty—these belong to the True Order of things;

they are of the texture of the universe; of these is the divine Garment of Life woven. Pure Religion is glad, not gloomy. It is Light without darkness or shadow.

Despondency, disappointment, grief—these are the reflex aspects of pleasurable excitement, self-seeking, and desire. Give up the latter, and the former will forever disappear; then there remains the perfect Bliss of Heaven.

Abounding and unalloyed Happiness is man's true life; perfect Blessedness is his rightful portion; and when he loses his false life and finds the true he enters into the full possession of his Kingdom. The Kingdom of Heaven is man's Home; and it is here and now, it is in his own heart, and he is not left without Guides, if he wills to find it. All man's sorrows and sufferings are the result of his own self-elected estrangement from the Divine Source, the All-Good, the Father, the Heart of Love. Let him return to his Home; his peace awaits him.

The Heavenly-hearted are without sorrow and suffering, because they are without sin. What the worldly-minded call *troubles* they regard as pleasant tasks of Love and Wisdom. Troubles belong to hell; they do not enter Heaven. This is so simple it should not appear strange. If you have a trouble it is in your own mind, and nowhere else; you make it, it is not made for you; it is not in your task; it is not in that outward thing. You are its creator, and it derives its life from you only. Look upon all your difficulties as lessons to be learned, as aids to spiritual growth, and lo! they are difficulties no longer! This is one of the Pathways up to Heaven.

To transmute everything into Happiness and Joy, this is supremely the work and duty of the Heavenly-minded man. To reduce everything to wretchedness and deprivation is the process which the worldly-minded unconsciously pursue. To live in Love is to work in Joy. Love is the magic that transforms all things into power and beauty. It brings plenty out of poverty, power out of weakness, loveliness out of deformity, sweetness out of bitterness, light out of darkness, and produces all blissful conditions out of its own substantial but indefinable essence.

He who loves can never want. The universe belongs to Goodness, and it therefore belongs to the good man. It can be possessed by all without stint or shrinking, for Goodness, and the abundance of Goodness (material, mental, and spiritual abundance), is inexhaustible. Think lovingly, speak lovingly, act lovingly, and your every need shall be supplied; you shall not walk in desert places, and no danger shall overtake you.

Love sees with faultless vision, judges true judgment, acts in wisdom. Look through the eyes of Love, and you shall see everywhere the Beautiful and True; judge with the mind of Love, and you shall err not, shall wake no wail of sorrow; act in the spirit of Love, and you shall strike undying harmonies upon the Harp of Life..

Make no compromise with self. Cease not to strive until your whole being is swallowed up in Love. To love all and always—this is the Heaven of heavens. "Let there be nothing within thee that is not very beautiful and very gentle, and then will be nothing without thee that is not beautiful and softened by the spell of thy presence."

All that you do, let it be done in calm wisdom, and not from desire, impulse, or opinion; this is the Heavenly way of action.

Purify your thought-world until no stain is left, and you will ascend into Heaven while living in the body. You will then see the things of the outward world clothed in all beautiful forms. Having found the Divine Beauty within ourselves, it springs to life in every outward thing. To the beautified soul the world is beautiful.

Undeveloped souls are merely unopened flowers. The perfect Beauty lies concealed within, and will one day reveal itself to the full-orbed light of Heaven. Seeing men thus, we stand where evil is not, and where the eye beholds only good. Herein lies the peace and patience and beauty of Love—*it sees no evil*. He who loves thus becomes the protector of all men. Though in their ignorance they should hate him, he shields and loves them.

What gardener is so foolish as to condemn his flowers because they do not develop in a day? Learn to love, and you shall see in all souls, even those called "degraded," the Divine Beauty, and shall know that it will not fail to come forth in its own season. This is one of the Heavenly Visions; it is out of this that Gladness comes.

Sin, sorrow, suffering—these are the dark gropings of the unopened soul for Light. Open the petals of your soul and let the glorious Light stream in.

Every sinful soul is an unresolved harmony. It shall at last strike the Perfect Chord, and swell the joyful melodies of Heaven.

Hell is the preparation for Heaven; and out of

the debris of its ruined hovels are built pleasant mansions wherein the perfected soul may dwell.

Night is only a fleeting shadow which the world casts, and sorrow is but a transient shade cast by the self. "Come out into the Sunlight." Know this, O reader! that you are divine. You are not cut off from the Divine except in your own unbelief. Rise up, O Son of God! and shake off the nightmare of sin which binds you; accept your heritage—the Kingdom of Heaven! Drug your soul no longer with the poisons of false beliefs. You are not "a worm of the dust" unless you choose to make yourself one. You are a divine, immortal, God-born being, and this you may know if you will to seek and find. Cling no longer to your impure and grovelling thoughts, and you shall know that you are a radiant and celestial spirit, filled with all pure and lovable thoughts. Wretchedness and sin and sorrow are not your portion here unless you accept them as such; and if you do this, they will be your portion hereafter, for these things are not apart from your soul-condition; they will go wherever you go; they are only within you.

Heaven, not hell, is your portion here and always. It only requires you to take that which belongs to you. You are the master, and you choose whom you will serve. You are the maker of your state, and your choice determines your condition. What you pray and ask for (with your mind and heart, not with your lips merely), this you receive. You are served as you serve. You are conditioned as you condition. You garner in your own.

Heaven is yours; you have but to enter in and

take possession; and Heaven means Supreme Happiness, Perfect Blessedness; it leaves nothing to be desired; nothing to be grieved over. It is complete satisfaction *now and in this world.* It is within you; and if you do not know this, it is because you persist in turning the back of your soul upon it. *Turn round* and you shall behold it.

Come and live in the sunshine of your being. Come out of the shadows and the dark places. You are framed for Happiness. You are a child of Heaven. Purity, Wisdom, Love, Plenty, Joy, and Peace—these are the eternal Realities of the Kingdom, and they are yours, but you cannot possess them in sin; they have no part in the Realm of Darkness. They belong to ''the Light which lighteth every man that cometh into the world,'' the Light of spotless Love. They are the heritage of the holy Christ Child who shall come to birth in your soul when you are ready to divest yourself of all your impurities. They are your real self.

But he whose soul has been safely delivered of the Wonderful Joy-Child does not forget the travail of the world.